DATE DUE 2/02

GAYLORD			PRINTED IN U.S.A.

SandCastle 3

Homophones

Can You Hear Me From Here?

Amanda Rondeau

Publishing Company

JACKSON COUNTY LIBRARY SERVICES
MEDFORD, OREGON 97501

Published by SandCastle™, an imprint of ABDO Publishing Company, 4940 Viking Drive, Edina, Minnesota 55435.

Library of Congress Cataloging-in-Publication Data

Rondeau, Amanda, 1974-
   Can you hear me from here? / Amanda Rondeau.
      p. cm. -- (Homophones)
   Includes index.
   Summary: Photographs and simple text introduce homophones, words that sound alike but are spelled differently and have different meanings.
   ISBN 1-57765-780-2
   1. English language--Homonyms--Juvenile literature. [1. English language--Homonyms.] I. Title. II. Series.

PE1595 .R67 2002
428.1--dc21

2001053310

The SandCastle concept, content, and reading method have been reviewed and approved by a national advisory board including literacy specialists, librarians, elementary school teachers, early childhood education professionals, and parents.

Let Us Know

After reading the book, SandCastle would like you to tell us your stories about reading. What is your favorite page? Was there something hard that you needed help with? Share the ups and downs of learning to read. We want to hear from you! To get posted on the ABDO Publishing Company Web site, send us email at:

sandcastle@abdopub.com

About SandCastle™

Nonfiction books for the beginning reader

- Basic concepts of phonics are incorporated with integrated language methods of reading instruction. Most words are short, and phrases, letter sounds, and word sounds are repeated.

- Book levels are based on the ATOS™ for Books formula. Other considerations for readability include the number of words in each sentence, the number of characters in each word, and word lists based on curriculum frameworks.

- Full-color photography reinforces word meanings and concepts.

- "Words I Can Read" list at the end of each book teaches basic elements of grammar, helps the reader recognize the words in the text, and builds vocabulary.

- Reading levels are indicated by the number of flags on the castle.

SandCastle uses the following definitions for this series:

- Homographs: words that are spelled the same but sound different and have different meanings. *Easy memory tip: "-graph"= same look*

- Homonyms: words that are spelled and sound the same but have different meanings. *Easy memory tip: "-nym"= same name*

- Homophones: words that sound alike but are spelled differently and have different meanings. *Easy memory tip: "-phone"= sound alike*

Look for more SandCastle books in these three reading levels:

Level 1 (one flag)	**Level 2** (two flags)	**Level 3** (three flags)

Grades Pre-K to K 5 or fewer words per page	**Grades K to 1** 5 to 10 words per page	**Grades 1 to 2** 10 to 15 words per page

hear

to sense sounds;
to listen to
something

here

at or in
this place

Homophones are words that sound alike but are spelled differently and have different meanings.

Missy plays the flute and Jake plays the piano.

I like to hear their music.

My family is here in the backyard.

We pose for a picture.

Airplanes are loud.

You can hear some of them from the ground.

We have a potato sack race
here in the sand.

Ted can only hear the tractor.

It is very loud.

We told Curly to come here for his bath.

There are many fans at the game.

We can hear them cheer loudly.

It snows here in Maine.

We like to build snowmen.

I feel happy with my friend.

It is fun to hear him laugh.

We build sand castles here at the beach.

It is fun to work together.

Ben likes to hear his flute.

He practices every day.

Naomi was lost and asked for directions.

He said to turn here at the corner.

I can hear Jim yelling in my ear.

He really likes the slide.

Janie and Carlos are my best friends.

I like being here with them.

Megan loves the farm.

She comes here to pet the cows.

What do you hear when we sing in the choir?

(songs)

Words I Can Read

Nouns

A noun is a person, place, or thing

airplanes (AIR-planez)
p. 8
backyard (BAK-yard)
p. 7
bath (BATH) p. 11
beach (BEECH) p. 15
choir (KWIRE) p. 21
corner (KOR-nur) p. 17
cows (KOUZ) p. 20
day (DAY) p. 16
directions
(duh-REK-shuhnz)
p. 17
ear (IHR) p. 18
family (FAM-uh-lee)
p. 7

fans (FANZ) p. 12
farm (FARM) p. 20
flute (FLOOT) pp. 6, 16
friend (FREND) p. 14
friends (FRENDZ) p. 19
game (GAME) p. 12
ground (GROUND) p. 8
homophones
(HOME-uh-fonez)
p. 5
meanings (MEE-ningz)
p. 5
music (MYOO-zik) p. 6
piano (pee-AN-oh) p. 6
picture (PIK-chur) p. 7
place (PLAYSS) pp. 4, 9

potato (puh-TAY-toh)
p. 9
race (RAYSS) p. 9
sack (SAK) p. 9
sand (SAND) p. 9
sand castles (SAND
KASS-uhlz) p. 15
slide (SLIDE) p. 18
snowmen (SNOH-men)
p. 13
songs (SAWNGZ) p. 21
sounds (SOUNDZ) p. 4
tractor (TRAK-tur) p. 10
words (WURDZ) p. 5

Proper Nouns

A proper noun is the name
of a person, place, or thing

Ben (BEN) p. 16
Carlos (KAR-lohs) p. 19
Curly (KUR-lee) p. 11
Jake (JAYK) p. 6
Janie (JAY-nee) p. 19

Jim (JIM) p. 18
Maine (MAYN) p. 13
Megan (MAY-guhn)
p. 20
Missy (MISS-ee) p. 6

Naomi (nay-OH-mee)
p. 17
Ted (TED) p. 10

22

Pronouns

A pronoun is a word that replaces a noun

he (HEE) pp. 16, 17, 18
him (HIM) p. 14
I (EYE) pp. 6, 14, 18, 19
it (IT) pp. 10, 13, 14, 15
she (SHEE) p. 20

something
   (SUHM-thing) p. 4
them (THEM)
   pp. 8, 12, 19
there (THAIR) p. 12

we (WEE) pp. 7, 9, 11,
   12, 13, 15, 21
what (WUHT) p. 21
you (YOO) pp. 8, 21

Verbs

A verb is an action or being word

are (AR) pp. 5, 8, 12, 19
asked (ASKD) p. 17
being (BEE-ing) p. 19
build (BILD) pp. 13, 15
can (KAN)
   pp. 8, 10, 12, 18
cheer (CHIHR) p. 12
come (KUHM) p. 11
comes (KUHMZ) p. 20
do (DOO) p. 21
feel (FEEL) p. 14
have (HAV) pp. 5, 9

hear (HIHR) pp. 4, 6, 8,
   10, 12, 14, 16, 18, 21
is (IZ) pp. 7, 10, 14, 15
laugh (LAF) p. 14
like (LIKE) pp. 6, 13, 19
likes (LIKESS) pp. 16, 18
listen (LISS-uhn) p. 4
loves (LUHVZ) p. 20
pet (PET) p. 20
plays (PLAYZ) p. 6
pose (POHZ) p. 7
practices
   (PRAK-tiss-ez) p. 16

said (SED) p. 17
sense (SENSS) p. 4
sing (SING) p. 21
snows (SNOHZ) p. 13
sound (SOUND) p. 5
spelled (SPELD) p. 5
told (TOHLD) p. 11
turn (TURN) p. 17
was (WUHZ) p. 17
work (WURK) p. 15
yelling (YEL-ing) p. 18

Adjectives

An adjective describes something

alike (uh-LIKE) p. 5
best (BEST) p. 19
different (DIF-ur-uhnt) p. 5
fun (FUHN) pp. 14, 15

happy (HAP-ee) p. 14
his (HIZ) pp. 11, 16
lost (LOST) p. 17
loud (LOUD) pp. 8, 10
many (MEN-ee) p. 12

my (MYE) pp. 7, 14, 18, 19
some (SUHM) p. 8
their (THAIR) p. 6
this (THISS) p. 4

Adverbs

An adverb tells how, when, or where something happens

differently (DIF-ur-uhnt-lee) p. 5
every (EV-ree) p. 16

here (HIHR) pp. 4, 7, 9, 11, 13, 15, 17, 19, 20
loudly (LOUD-lee) p. 12
only (OHN-lee) p. 10

really (REE-lee) p. 18
together (tuh-GETH-ur) p. 15
very (VER-ee) p. 10

24